Challenges of Life
and THE FRUIT *of*
THE HOLY SPIRIT

Kathy Lee

WESTBOW
PRESS®
A DIVISION OF THOMAS NELSON
& ZONDERVAN

This book is a work of non-fiction. Unless otherwise noted, the author and the publisher make no explicit guarantees as to the accuracy of the information contained in this book and in some cases, names of people and places have been altered to protect their privacy.

WestBow Press books may be ordered through booksellers or by contacting:

WestBow Press
A Division of Thomas Nelson & Zondervan
1663 Liberty Drive
Bloomington, IN 47403
www.westbowpress.com
844-714-3454

Scripture taken from the New King James Version® Copyright © 1982 by Thomas Nelson. Used by permission. All rights reserved.

ISBN: 978-1-6642-6711-4 (sc)
ISBN: 978-1-6642-6710-7 (e)

Print information available on the last page.

WestBow Press rev. date: 05/21/2022

A Gift for:

From: _____

Date: _____

Galatians 5:22-23
But the Fruits of the Spirit is
Love, Joy, Peace, Kindness, Goodness,
Faithfulness, Gentleness and Self-Control

Contents

Foreword xi
Psalm 121 xiii
Introduction xv

Love 1
Children 17
Communication 31
Finances 51
Peace 65
Patience. 71
Faithfulness 77
Self-Control. 83
Joy. 93
Long-Suffering. 99
Kindness 105
Goodness. 111
Gentleness 117

Friends 123
Forgiveness. 131
Notes 137
The Author 139

Foreword

This book is being written whilst going through challenges in my life and how it aligns with some of the Fruits of the Holy Spirit.
I thank God that He is my source and my strength.

If God is all I have then He is all I need!

This book was written with the spirit of the word: Psalm 121
I will lift up my eyes to the hills.
Through challenges I reached out to God.
He sent me a word for every step I had to take.
The steps were steep, the turns were sharp, I had to overcome the fear of spiritual heights.

More importantly I learned that we need to be very wary of the prayers we say for ourselves.
As there is a saying be careful of what you wish for, well there is a saying be careful of what you pray for.

I want to thank my Sister Geselle who pushed me to write this book. I love you Sis!
Thanks to my prayer warriors: Geselle; Simone; Hilde; Roxanne and Donna.
Let us continue to fight the good fight of faith.

Psalm 121

I will lift up my eyes to the hills
From whence cometh my help?
My help comes from the Lord,
Who made heaven and earth.

He will not allow your foot to be moved;
He who keeps you will not slumber,
Behold He who keeps Israel,
Shall neither slumber nor sleep.

The Lord is your keeper,
The Lord is your shade at your right hand.
The sun shall not strike you by day,
Nor the moon by night.

The Lord shall preserve you from all evil;
He shall preserve your soul.
The Lord shall preserve your coming in
From this time forth, and even forevermore.

Introduction

Life has so many challenges. Most of my challenges were always of a spiritual nature.

I often asked God why me? Why do I have to go through these challenges?

Then one day I read: Don't ask: Why me, say instead Try Me! Life's experiences should always teach to be Better not Bitter.

I decided one day to start reading my bible. I had no idea of how to read my bible or if there is a method.

Apparently, there is a method for reading bible. But I did not go to any school of theology I just picked it up and started from the beginning – Genesis 1. The creation.

I pray before I read. I ask God to give me revelation of His word. I ask Him to show me what He wants me to know, more importantly what are You teaching me?

Do you know that absolutely everything in and about life is written in the bible?

There is so much to learn from this book. Whatever the challenges we have, the solution is in the bible.

Do you know that there are 66 books – In the Old Testament there are 39 books and in the New Testament there are 27 books.

An important lesson I learnt also is that God operates in times and seasons.

One never knows how long a season can be. It can be one day, one week, one month, one year or it can be years! What is important, I have learnt, is that for every challenge there is a word in season or your Raema word. The key in our seasons is how obedient we need to be and how to learn the lessons God is teaching and showing us. More importantly is to Worship Him regardless of the season.

If we are not pliable to His word and lessons it determines in part the length of the season.

Genesis shows us that the journey the Israelites took lasted 40 years which in essence should have only taken 11 days. Deuteronomy 1:2 gave the GPS of that mapping!

The Israelites took 40 years because of rebellion and disobedience to God. They forgot all the blessings they received from God. They murmured and were disgruntled.

I would also like to add my perspective which is: They lacked maturity, understanding, gratefulness; the right attitude and wisdom.

Love

1 Corinthian 13:4-7

Love suffers long and is kind; love does not envy; love does not parade itself; is not puffed up; does not behave rudely; does not seek its own, is not provoked, thinks no evil; does not rejoice in iniquity, but rejoices in the truth; bears all things; believes all things; hopes all things; endures all things.

Love never fails.

Challenges in Life: LOVE

The essence of God and who He is, is LOVE.
God says if we can't love then we are not of Him!
Love can be very challenging.

The Love between Husband and wife.
This out of all the different types of love is the most challenging.
Most times it's challenging because we are unevenly yoked. The bible speaks about this in 2 Corinthians 6:14. It makes life harder. But God can make it work if both parties are pliable and want the promises of God. I would also advise to seek counsel with your pastor, and both do marriage counseling before the wedding.
My personal belief is that sometimes an unevenly yoked marriage is God's way of using one to bring salvation to another. It's not God's word, but I do know that it's not His will that any of us perish, but have eternal life – John 3:16
Unevenly yoked is two people coming together, sometimes from different backgrounds and cultures with different religious beliefs.
When it's not ordained by God and if God is not between them both, then chances of survival of this union is almost nil.

God appointed the husband to be King and Priest of the home.

A woman came out of man's rib.
Not from his feet to be walked on.
Not from his head to be superior
But from his side to be equal in support.
Under his arm to be protected and next to his
heart to be loved.
(Author unknown)

The wife is called to stand at his side in submission and as proverbs 31:15 says the wife rises whilst it's still night and provides food for her household!

Wives are supposed to be the strength and honor. Our mouths are to be filled with wisdom and our tongues is the law of kindness.

Proverbs 14:1 says: A wise woman builds her home, but the foolish one tears it down! This means that we should stay away from gossip and ill speaking our husbands. Use our words to build our husbands. Our words must be soft and kind. Even if we are angry. Ephesians 4:26 tells us that we can be angry, but sin not; and do not let the sun go down on our anger, and do not make room for the devil. That's what we do in anger – make room for the devil to come in.

As women we are not to eat the bread of idleness.

Idle hands are the devil's workshop.

Men ought to love their wives as Christ loves the church and gave Himself (Ephesians 5:25)!

Genesis 2:24 says that men ought to leave his father and mother and cleave to his wife and become one flesh.

Men you can't give your all to your wife, if you are still cleaving to your past, your parents your single life and single friends. That's why it says leave and cleave.

You must leave and now build a new life that God has blessed you with.

An area that I believe should not be a part of your life as a couple, is the boys' night out or girls' night out! That's for the single life! It should now be *our* night out. I am hearing a great deal of disagreement with this. But may I tell you that's a recipe for disaster.

As a couple it is very important to find common goals, find entertainment together as a couple – the movies, dinner, the beach, a picnic; just spend time together. Hold each other's hands when walking.

You should now be with friends that are couples and fellowship together. This makes a very healthy way of life for you as a couple. Your friends should be able to support you both and carry the same ideals and belief system.

Ask God to send friends into your lives. Friends that can give Godly counsel, friends that are wise and that can give good solid wise advice.

The argument was that each need space and time away from each other. You get that when you are at your respective jobs. You can get that if one wants to read and the other doing something around the house.

One of the best things between a married couple is the ability to call each other during the day, check in on each other, meet for lunch and it doesn't have to be expensive! If not lunch, meet each other after work for a small bite or ice cream or a drink.

Whatever you do make it happen. As a couple, you should always be walking in the same direction. Couples complement each other. No one is better than the other; you both bring equally to the table; and this does not mean financially. It's emotionally, spiritually, and physically.

We are responsible for our own happiness. My husband is not responsible for my happiness and vice versa. This is what I mean by complementing each other.
My happiness comes from being at peace with myself, loving myself, taking care of me mentally, emotionally, and physically. Likewise, the husband must do the same. It's a fallacy that we are responsible for another person's happiness.

Trust and communication are very important elements in a marriage. There must be no secrets, no lies. This is explained in detail in another chapter.
Truth is of the utmost importance. You both discuss everything with each other, not outside parties. Outside parties are not privy to what's going on in your home, so they can't be objective, and they hear one side of the story. Some believe that not everything should be discussed with your partner, not everything your partner should know. This just encourages deceit into the marriage.
I have heard many couples talk about keeping separate finances. I believe that if the two of us are together and we are building a life together, then there should be a main account, and both are aligned as to how the financial expenses are to be shared. I also believe that each person should have their own personal accounts for your personal needs. But it should never be done with the spirit of distrust and lies and the hiding of finances.

For God to bless your finances as a couple, tithes and offerings is a must and we see this in both Malachi 3:10 – 11, and Luke 6:38 says It will be given to us full measure, 2 Corinthians 9:6-8 speaks of sowing seeds and giving.

Be aligned with each other on your spending; savings; what you put towards a vacation; buying a home and education for when children enter the union.

Adhering to these laws ensures that we will never lack for anything, as God is our source and provider.

When we honor Him with our finances, He rebukes the devourer of our harvest.

Clear and precise communication. Both must try to be on the same page. Agree to disagree. No two are alike. But certainly, a compromise can be agreed upon.

Always pray and ask God for your spirits to be aligned so that you both can make decisions with wisdom.

When there are issues and they will arise, discuss them together in a very calm environment.

If one is angry, let that person calm down as when words are said in the heat of the moment they can never be retracted. Too late the spoken word did damage.

Key: don't let ill feelings fester. Think of an infected wound. Discuss what upsets you and try to work together to iron out the struggles. DO NOT GO TO BED ANGRY!

Ephesians 4:26-27 says Be angry and sin not; do not let the sun go down on your anger and give no opportunity to the devil.

Research from a university says:

Going to bed angry is a toxic pattern that causes long term damage. Your brain puts that experience into your long-term memory zones while you are sleeping. This causes the fight to hold lasting impressions and intensifies the anger.

From this you have the unforgiveness seeping in. We ought to forgive and let it go. Do not hold on to anger and the cause of the anger. Unforgiveness makes a person bitter.

The challenge for men and women comes from not following the laws of God.

Husband and wives want to both control each other with everything from finances to children. That is not how the Lord ordained it to be.

Psalm 127:1 says: Unless the Lord builds a house, they labor in vain.

Women think that in submission we must stoop and bow down, but may I tell you that in submission we do have greater control.

1 Peter 3:1 says *that without a word the men can be won just by our conduct.*

Likewise, husbands should be kind and understanding to their wives, they must give honor to their wives so that they can enjoy the blessings of God and prosper unhindered.

Husbands, protect your wives. Always have her back, especially in the presence of company, even if she's wrong. Behind closed doors discuss the situation.

Wives, likewise, protect your husbands and his character.

Don't ill speak each other with outsiders. If there are problems and it can't be dealt with between you both, then seek counseling from someone you both trust who can be very objective and not take sides. This is not a competition. Someone who can give Godly counsel and steer you both on the right path.

Someone that would encourage healing and forgiveness. Start with your Pastor.

In these modern times we have strayed so far from the word of God, that is why the divorce rate is so high. As a couple we no longer have God at the center of our lives.

Most times the women are carrying the home and marriage spiritually instead of the men.

The couple that prays together, stays together!

Fellowship with others. Church attendance is vitally important to you both as a couple and eventually as parents. You can always get the support through this avenue should you need counseling.

Men have become so hard and rebellious towards God. They have hardened their hearts; they believe that to love God and follow Him is being weak. That's a lie from the pit of hell. A strong man loves and obeys God and takes the mantle up as the priest of his home. Happy wife, happy life!

This is not to say, that some women do emasculate their husbands and take control of the home. This is especially if she is either the breadwinner or earns more than the husband.

Women, please note that when you do this, you are stepping out from under the covering of your husband. When you step out from under his covering, you are giving the devil the legal right to attack your home. How can this happen you ask?

Think about an open umbrella. If you step out from under it, it's either you get burnt in the sun or wet in the rain.

You will see that you can no longer see your way financially. Everything that can go wrong will go wrong, things in the home will start to fall apart emotionally. More fights and arguments. Where there was peace there is now discord, health issues, children's needs become greater as the house is filled with anxiety.

The devil attacks families. It's a priority for the devil to attack homes.

Strife and confusion steps in, the house is filled with turmoil. As the home becomes filled with animosity and discord, when men see the struggles and the constant bickering, they leave. They find a place where they are comfortable, where it's peaceful and where they think they are happy, and they go. Unfortunately, it's always into the arms of another woman, who has been waiting and lurking in the shadows. Little do the men know that the grass is not greener. A myth, a lie!

Put all your energy into the healing of the marriage unless there is a threat to one's life, go to therapy.

God hates divorce. Malachi 2:16

Reconciliation and restoration will always be God's word and plan. He will restore if you ask Him to.

As a family unit, a family bond is very strong and a force to be reckoned with, especially if the family has Christ at the center. Pray that He binds you with cords of love that can't be broken.

Pray that your union and your home be protected by God.

Find time as a couple to fast together.

You must both agree to when you both shall fast. At least once a week. It strengthens you both spiritually and solidifies your relationship as a couple and in one with God.

Remember in Unity we can achieve more. As a couple living in unity we exert tremendous power, as united prayer is powerful. God loves and blesses unity.

There is power in agreement. Matthew 18:19 says if two agree as touching anything that they ask, it shall be done. Now that's the powerful promise of God!

For a home to prosper and flourish Unity must be present.

Challenges of being married to an unsaved spouse

There are challenges to being married to an unsaved spouse. But nothing is too difficult for God. As indicated earlier, sometimes God will align you with an unsaved partner because He wants that person's salvation. It's important to God that none of us perish. God sees something in that person that a spouse nor the outside world can see.

This is not to say we should go out and look for unsaved persons to marry. Always seek God's face for approval and answers.

The challenges lie with the belief system. Just know that it will be a constant battle for that spouse's soul. The devil will not give up. It takes a lot of consistent, constant prayer and fasting. You must go before God and counter-petition for that soul. Just as the devil counter-petitioned for Job. You must go and continuously pray and fast until your spouse's salvation.

There are numerous scriptures you can declare over them. The main scripture I say over my family comes from Joshua 24:15 - As for me and my home we will serve The Lord. God didn't promise one or some. He promised ALL.

We must stand on God's word and His promises in faith. Despite what we see.

Because faith is the substance of things hoped for, the evidence of things not yet seen (Hebrews 11:1).

There's a saying we must stoop to conquer. We must be submissive, just as the bible instructed in the case of a saved wife.

We must be submissive, that if any of them be disobedient to the word, they may be won without a word from us, but will be won by our behavior. This means that we must not nag. We need to go to our prayer closet and fight for them spiritually. That's where our battles are won. Not in an argument.

Most unevenly yoked marriages are where the wife is saved not the husbands.

God expects us to be a biblical wife. This is outlined in Proverbs 31:10-31. The Virtuous Wife.

We must love unconditionally, be compassionate and lead from behind. It's hard work but remember we signed on for that job when we knowingly married them.

If they attend church with you then half the battle is won. The word and the Holy Spirit will eventually bring change.

Invite them to attend service, but don't force them. In everything GO TO GOD. Let Him move and stir up their spirits. Without a word we can change them (1 Peter 3:1-2). They will not change if we continuously nag and beat them over the head. We can't force someone to love.

At times you will get tired as you see no change, but this is what we mean by having faith. Look to the goal and the prize, not what is directly in front of you.

Submission needs trust, trust comes from love.

My behavior is NOT dependent upon my husband. My behavior must exemplify God's word and what God expects of me as the saved wife.

Fast and pray. Even if we go before God in the wee hours of the morning on our faces. Then that is what we must do. There are scriptures you can declare over them. Take them and personalize them.

Some of these scriptures as follows:

- Ephesians 5:28 Husbands ought to love their wives as Christ love the church and gave himself.
- Proverbs 5:15 & 19
- 1 Peter 4:8 That we continue to love each other.
- Ephesians 4:32 – That we be kind to each other, tenderhearted, forgiving each other, just as God.
- 1 Peter 3:7 – That husband must honor his wife.
- Matthew 19:6 – What God has joined together, let no man put asunder.

These are just some of the scriptures that you can personalize and declare over your husband and by extension the marriage.

There is a movie I can highly recommend for you as a wife to watch – The War Room.

For a husband with an unsaved wife – Fireproof.

Stand strong in your faith, that God will deliver. He never fails. That's the only thing God can't do – fail.

It Takes a Trial to experience a Triumph. (Words taken from the Reality show Basketball Wives).

To end this, for a marriage to work there must be Trust, Loyalty, fidelity and LOVE.

Above all God MUST be at the centre!

Prayer over your marriage

Heavenly Father, we come before you in repentance for sinful words, sinful thoughts and sinful deeds.

We come to You, as husband & wife thanking You for each other, thanking You for Your protective hand over us. Thanking You for providing for us and our family.

May we always keep You at the center of us as a couple and as parents.

May we always walk in obedience to You and Your word.

We pray Lord to love You, and to be loving to each other.

Let us be always quick to forgive, be faithful to each other as we pray for our marriage bed to be undefiled. Keep us away from all temptation.

Keep us in the secret shelter of Your wings, protecting us from our enemies.

Teach us Your ways Oh Lord, that we may always be obedient, compassionate, and humble.

Strengthen and sustain us, guide us, fill us with Your Holy Spirit and keep us attuned to the move of Your Spirit.

Let our spirits be aligned so that we can make decisions together with wisdom.

Let our communication be filled with love and that we listen to each other in patience instead of blame.

Help us both to build a happy home filled with Love, Joy, laughter, and peace.

We pray that You surround us with true Godly friends and friendships.

We pray that our family will always follow You in obedience.

We come against lack in our home as we look to You as our source and provider.

We pray this in Jesus' mighty name,

AMEN.

Pray and declare the blessings of Deuteronomy 28:3-14 over your lives and family. (Personalize it).

Children

Isaiah 54:13
All your children shall be taught by the Lord,
and great shall be their peace.

Proverbs 22:6
Train up a child in the way he should go.
Even when he is old, he will not depart from it.

Challenges of Love between parents and children

Psalm 127:3 – Behold Children are a gift from the Lord. The fruit of the womb is a reward.

Children are always a blessing from God. So why then as parents we are quick to individually leave and break up our families and have the children raised in single family homes? When you buy a new car, you do everything to make sure you take care of that car. Why can't it be the same with your children?

Children are to be nourished, nurtured, and loved by parents. It should be every parent's priority to make sure their home is comfortable and there is an abundance of love so that children can thrive and grow and be happy and contented.

All couples at some point have disagreements. When that happens, we must never include the children in the argument, and we must never ill speak the other parent! Never make them choose sides. It's unhealthy to you both and to the children.

They must also never hear you ill speak other family members. Adults' business has no right in children's business.

A happy child will always do well academically and contribute to society in a meaningful way.

As parents we are to love them, teach them to love God, make sure that church is a necessary part of ALL your lives. Teach them how to be respectful, how to be forgiving, how to love, how to share; among many other areas that create a well-balanced life for each child. Discipline them when needed but do so with love.

There must be NO favoritism if there is more than one child. They each have different personalities and must be given the same love in different ways.

They need to be respected no matter their ages. Respect given is respect earned.

Children have the right to be respected. I have witnessed parents bully their children, call them derogatory names, demean them, demotivate them, put them down and crush their self- esteem. No child deserves that treatment!

God blessed everyone with a talent, a gift. It's up to us as a parent to help that child to discover what is his/her talent and nurture it. Let them grow and thrive.

The bible has many scriptures that you can use as affirmations over their lives.

Some parents try to control their children and use them to live their life vicariously through them. It's not your life, it's theirs. You had your chance. Now it's their turn.

Don't steal their opportunities, don't make them do what they are not equipped to do. Don't stifle them. Don't force what is not in their personality. In essence you are making them into handicaps.

Granted some children need your guidance, but you can't make them like what you like. Likewise, don't force them to be who they are not. They also can't be like Mrs. Jones' son. You are controlling them which leads to them being dependent on you as they haven't been taught to be independent thinkers. They can't function on their own. In other words, you have an emotionally paralyzed child.

Loving your child/children means we sometimes need to make harsh decisions for them, and this is part of their growth. If it is done in the right spirit, and it contributes to their wellbeing.

Giving a child a false sense of being better than anyone else can also be damaging to that child.

You are teaching that child that everyone else is wrong and you are right. Everyone is jealous of you.

You are developing that child to have a very false sense of security and to become haughty.

All these things you do as a parent is not love. You are destroying your child's life and not preparing them for the world outside. A world that is cruel and harsh.

They learn by example, and what they see. Teach the right thing, do the right thing!

Do you realize as parents we teach our children to lie? I noticed that during a very simple incident.

The telephone rang at home, and I told my son *if it's this person, tell them I am not home. Son proceeded to tell the person that I was not at home. Simple and small, isn't it?*

A few days after there was another incident with my son and I told him lying is wrong and he should not lie. *The answer back was*

"but you told me to lie when the person called".

Ouch! I walked into that!

I had to apologize to my son, and I also had to call the person and apologize. That lesson had to be taught if trust had to be built in our home and everyone had to be trusted.

The bible says in Proverbs 22:6 Train up a child in the way he should go, and when he gets old, he will not depart from it. Isaiah 54:13 says Let the children be taught by the Lord so that great shall be their peace.

It's also important as parents that we grow with them and learn with them. Be their biggest cheerleaders. Be present in every area of their lives, be a part of their activities, always be interested in their academics. What are they being taught, what are they learning, know the friends with whom they associate.

As parents we must always pray with them at night and before sending them to school.

Declare God's word over their lives. Ask the Holy Spirit for a foundational scripture for each child and have it painted in their bedroom and have them say it over their lives. Let it become a part of them.

Important, make sure that you can give them a good education.

Instill in them values and morals and prepare them for the world.

We must all leave the world (our sphere in which we live) a better place.

Teach them to be kind and empathetic towards others without being used. Let them know that in life there are also boundaries.

Teach them respect, the importance of being humble, gentle, kind towards others.

Let them know that those acts are not always reciprocated, but they should never allow it to change their character and who they were brought up to be.

Some prayer affirmations you can personalize and say over their lives:

John 1:12 - I am a child of God
Genesis 1:27 – God created me in His own image and likeness
Isaiah 43:1 – I belong to God, He called me by name, I am His.
Ephesians 2:10 – I am God's masterpiece.
Phillipians 4:13 – I can do all things through Christ, who strengthens me.
Jeremiah 29:11 – God has great plans for me.
Isaiah 54:13 – Let the children be taught by the Lord, so that great shall be their peace.

God says if we lack wisdom ask for it. (James 1:5)
Declare over them that they are wise because they have the wisdom of God.

These are just a few. There are so many scriptures, and you can teach them either one each week whatever way is easy for them to remember.
Another great way is to place these on a board or as an art board with their picture in the center and have the scriptures on the board, hung in their rooms.

Challenges of loving children that are not ours biologically

Children no matter where they come from deserve our love. **James 1:27** says to look after Orphans and widows in their distress, and to keep from being polluted by the world.

Often, children are brought into this world by uncaring parents. Even children that are born legitimately suffer through this.

1 Timothy 5:8 says if anyone does not provide for his household, he is worse than someone who does not believe in Jesus!

Children didn't ask to be brought into this world. As parents it is our responsibility when we bring them into the world to give each child a very fair and fighting chance.

When we adopt, we take full responsibility of the child as if they came from our own bodies!

No orphan should be treated as if they are our maids; that they should be in perpetual obligation to the new parents. They didn't ask or beg us to take them.

These need a lot of love and patience, as they would have come with that spirit of rejection. As they know they were abandoned by their parents and believe that they are not worthy of love.

It is our responsibility to feed them, clothe them, nurture them, teach them and train them up in the way they should go, so that they will not depart from that foundation.

Children learn what they see.

These children need a great deal of prayer and abundant love. They are broken, but we know that God is more than able to heal them. He will give you the strength as parents to love them and provide them with a safe and loving home.

Challenges of loving children that are not ours biologically

Children from blended families and orphans need to be constantly prayed for.

They are coming from one home into another, where both environments are totally different from what they are used to, so it is a process and a learning for all.

This takes a lot of time and loads of patience.

Children who are being blended into new families face difficulties adapting and accepting.

No matter their ages it is difficult for them to accept that this new or other person is now in the role of my mother/father.

Some depending on if the divorce was not amicable can be carrying the anger and bitterness for the parent that was left behind.

Parents jump into these new living conditions without proper counseling for themselves, the children, and the new "parent".

Boundaries need to be in place for both the child/children with the "new" parent.

Some children reject the new arrangements. Some of these rejections can be in subtle deceitfulness or tantrums, rebellion and lies. These children see how far they can go to either destroy the new marriage or see how they can get the parent to completely be on their side and push the other person out.

These issues must be dealt with if the home must have peace, joy, love, and laughter.

The children's welfare must be a priority, but not at the of the expense of the new marriage.

The children need to be counseled with until they are comfortable with the new living arrangements.

They must never be made to feel unaccepted.

You must never make them feel as if they don't belong. It must never be that's your child.

The child/children are now "OUR" child/children.

You must make the home OUR home.

This takes time and patience. But as a couple you must both be aligned in how to deal with and respond to the new arrangement. You must show the child/children a united front.

We are here as your parents, but you must live by our rules. Never show the child/children that you take their side over your spouse.

Children do know how to play one against the other and trust me they are masters at this art.

They pretend to love your new spouse but find a way to cause animosity and stir trouble.

They go as far as to master the art of getting deathly ill. They automatically become hypochondriacs. All because they want your full attention. They want to be the centre of your world and don't want you loving anyone else.

Prayer over your Children

Heavenly Father, we thank You for the gift of our child/children.

We pray that You would guide us to be good stewards over our child/children.

We pray that You surround our child/children with Godly friends and friendships.

Wherever You can use them to make a difference in lives God guide and protect them to do Your will.

Let them always be respectful to their elders, and to their peers.

We pray that they will always show kindness to others, that they have compassion towards those that are not as fortunate as they are.

Keep them humble Lord. We pray that their character will exemplify You.

We pray that they will be devoted to You and that their lives will have purpose and that they fulfill the destiny You have ordained for them.

Bless them with wisdom, knowledge and understanding of You and who You are.

Give them minds and tongues of the learned and hands as a pen of a ready writer.

We pray that they love school and learning new things. Place them with teachers that are kind and that will encourage and motivate them.

Let them ultimately be taught by You Lord so that great shall be their peace.

Guide and protect them and give them wisdom to make wise decisions.

Guide their footsteps; show them the path always. Warn them when they are about to make costly mistakes. Strengthen them to stand against temptation.

Protect them from falling into less than desirable company. Fill them with Your peace.

We pray this in Jesus' name,

Amen.

Communication

James 1:19
Know this my beloved brothers: let every person be quick to hear, slow to speak, slow to anger

Ephesians 4:29
Let no corrupt talk come out of your mouths, but only such as is good for building up, as it fits the occasion, that it may give grace to those who hear.

Challenges in Life: Communication

It has been said that God gave us two ears and one mouth for a reason.

In marriage you should open your ears to hear and listen to what your spouse is saying and open your eyes to how your spouse is saying it!

To often we hear, but are we listening to what is being said? In the chapter dealing with Love, I wrote about communication. But God wanted me to write in greater detail about communication. He sees it as important.

Many failed relationships are because of the lack of proper communication or miscommunication. There may be some repetition and I can only write what God placed on my heart.

What is communication?

The ability to communicate is a gift from God to enable us to develop relationships with others.

Webster's has communication as a process by which information is exchanged between individuals through a common system.

The dictionary's meaning felt cold to me.

I love how God sees it.

Whether you are a Christian or not, the bible gives some great wisdom and guidelines on communication.

2 Timothy 3:16 tells us that all scripture is inspired by God and profitable for teaching. It also warns us that what we say and how we say it is important to God.

Many of us are good at communication, some are not. I am not a great communicator, especially with those closest to me. I am great at communicating with those on the outside. Some people are talkers, and need to talk, whilst some people are quiet and like to keep everything private.

When putting this book together, I felt that this was just about challenges in life and that it was to be aligned with the Fruits of the spirit. When I thought I had completed the book, in the middle of the night God spoke and told me to include this portion as it is very important to Him.

He also told me what part of the book to place it.

The piece on Forgiveness was also important to Him.

So even though the Challenges of Life is aligned with the fruits, these two areas are important to God.

Challenges in Life: Communication

When we communicate, we communicate in different ways to different people.

How you communicate with your boss or co-worker is totally different to how you communicate with your spouse. (Even though some spouses may disagree with me).

How you communicate with your children is different to how you communicate with your spouse.

Important is that our communication should always have that underlying intonation of one of love. Yes, even if we are angry. As indicated earlier, it is always better to discuss the matter when our heads are calm, and all tempers are cooled. That way it's more productive.

Depending on who we are communicating with there is a difference in our language.

I will go through the differences of communication with different people.

Communicating with
your Spouse

The language we use to each other should always be of love. Communication in marriage is vitally important. I can't stress this enough.

The channels of communication must be open and clear. It must be meaningful and must have trust, respect and understanding. Your relationship will be better.

The moment you can't communicate it means that there is a level of fear and or mistrust.

This needs to be checked.

In some marriages, when there is abuse of any kind, it is difficult to communicate.

The abusive spouse has a mindset of being above correction and this comes from a spirit of pride. Abuse is not only physical, but also emotional. They are both equally as bad.

Having a spouse suffer emotional abuse damages not only the person's self-esteem but their mental faculties and psyche. Abuse in any form or fashion is never acceptable.

The abuser is a person of a very weak character.

When you must communicate with a spouse that's abusive one should have a third party involved. That third party must be a therapist, a pastor or someone that the person will accept and respect.

Spouses must treat each other with an abundant love, trust and respect and this goes for communication between the both of you. We are not always going to agree with each other, but we must always respect each other's opinion and perspective.

As a couple we are to be each other's best friend, we are to have that intimacy between us so that communication is easy. It is not a good practice to discuss what should be discussed with your spouse to "a friend."

All your hopes, your dreams, your plans should be discussed with your spouse, not a friend or an outsider.

If you are angry with your spouse it is not a good idea to discuss that anger and speak disparaging words about him/her to an outsider.

When communicating with our spouses there should be guidelines as to the process.

First, we must make the time for communication. Put aside daily chores and work. Put the kids to bed and then go into relax mode and make sure all electronics are switched off, including cell phones. There should be no interruptions, this is your time for each other to relax, unwind and talk to each other.

Leave the work outside the door unless it is an important part of the discussion.

When communicating, we need to be very specific, we can't go "globetrotting" with topics that are not relevant. This is where miscommunication starts. We start talking about the children and suddenly the neighbor and other random things are in the topic.

Be open with each other.

Blame game:
Try not to come off as blaming. This is not the blame game. Blame hurts not help.

If there is something that is upsetting you, chances are your spouse does not realize that what they are doing is upsetting you. I know sometimes it can be trivial, like not doing the dishes or leaving clothes on the floor of the bathroom. If you feel it's important to you, it's simple as "honey, my days are tiring, and you would be a great help if you can do the dishes". It may happen for the first few days then forgotten, but give the same communication: "Honey can you do the dishes?"

Respect/Disrespect:
No one likes to be disrespected. When you come at me in a disrespectful manner, I will not stay and listen.

We need to be respectful of the other person's feelings. We need to be a good listener. When we listen; when it's our turn to be heard we will get that same respect.

Disrespect is when the other person is speaking, you make derogatory comments, you smirk, you laugh at the person, you put down that person and make fun of them and trivialize what is important to them.

Nothing is solved and resolved. You end up with a discontented spouse, and this leaves the door open for distance and eventually they will find the ear that would listen. And it's not the ear you would want them talking with.

The bible clearly says that wives are to honor her husband so that he can fulfill his duties as head of the home. Likewise in **Ephesians 5:22-33** explains how we are to treat each other so clearly. Verse 33 says that husbands ought to love their wives as himself; and let the wife see that she respects her husband.

Nagging:
Sometimes we women can be nags. **Proverbs 21:9** says that it is better to live in the corner of the roof than in a house shared with a nagging and quarrelsome wife. Oh boy did I cringe at that! Are we that bad? To most men, Yes!!

I am not a therapist, and I can only research to see if there are ways to deal with a nagging wife. If I were to teach a woman how not to nag, I would advise that she reads **Proverbs 31**.
That scripture is very precise on what a perfect woman ought to be. As a woman, I try my best to be that example. Work hard, stay quiet, no idle hands and constantly prays for her household.
I have seen housewives who, as soon as husbands leave for work, and children off to school, they are parading the neighborhood and gossiping, or watching soap operas, and on the phone whole day.

Women who are idle will always be in the middle of confusion, and always know everybody's business.
Busy yourself in your home! I am not saying be a maid, but you can do the household chores, leave some for both husband and children to do, but find something worthwhile. Don't be that idle, gossiping person. Eventually that's what you would be known for.

Make a beautiful dinner, learn to bake, take online courses, there is always something to do.

I prefer to do all the chores, so it frees up the weekend where I can spend quality time with my family.

Nagging only makes your spouse feel inadequate. Nothing pleases you. It hurts and affects the relationship.

If a spouse has issues or need to complain about something, you need to listen, they brought it up because it's important to them. Don't get defensive about it. Listen and make the changes. By getting defensive, very soon they won't talk and just walk out.

Take it as constructive criticism where we can be better and have peace.

Remember we are not perfect and must be tolerant at times.

When expressing our feelings to each other, we should be mindful of not only expressing the negative but counter it with positive.

It's okay to express our fears, doubts and worries, but always include positive feelings.

Never forget to let your spouse know why you love them and keep reaffirming your love and commitment to them and your marriage.

As I said earlier, communication in a marriage is vitally import and it is important to keep the lines of communication open, honest, meaningful, respectful and above all communicate with love.

Prayer for Communication
with My Spouse

Heavenly father, I thank you for my spouse, thank you for our family, thank you for your presence in our lives.

Lord you said that we must always speak to each other in love. Help us to always communicate with each other the kingdom way.

Teach us to not only speak to each other with love, but let Your divine love stand between us so that we can set the example in our home.

Help us to be respectful to each other, let blame never play a part in our lives.

When there are issues in our lives, Lord, show us how to solve them with Your wisdom.

Give us that wisdom, love and understanding for each other.

Let our spirits be aligned so we can make decisions together in unity.

Keep temptation out of our marriage.

Help us to be good listeners and give us the right intonation. Let the Holy Spirit speak through us to each other.

This we ask in Jesus' name,
AMEN

Challenges in Life: Communication

Communication with Children

Colossians 3:21
Fathers, do not provoke your children, lest they become discouraged.

Ephesians 6:4
Fathers, do not exasperate your children but bring them up in the training and instruction of the Lord.

Challenges in Life: Communication

Communicating with children

In these modern times it's tough to communicate with children, especially in this age of technology.

Their heads are buried in the IPad, their phones, the television, and the other numerous devices that we give them. Heaven help us!

And if that wasn't enough, try communicating with them through the different ages and stages and phases of their lives.

Communicating with children takes great wisdom. The culture where I was raised, children were disciplined in ways that would now be seen as abuse. We were told to be respectful and with one look, we knew that we were doing something wrong.

In hindsight, we are better for it, did I go that route? No.

Children learn what they live, and if we set the right examples from the start, then we shouldn't have problems.

If as parents they see the examples of love in the relationship, that parents treat each other respectfully, that conversations take place to deal with issues, then they learn by these examples.

We can't be using foul language in the house and expect a child not to use that same language, or discipline them for using it. That's the tone we set.

A home filled will love and respect and the presence of God, is where we raise children in the way God expects. **Psalm 127:3** says that children are a blessing from the Lord. If they are a blessing, we should treat them as a gift from the Lord. With respect, with love and with great care.

Ephesians 6: 4 says that as parents we should not provoke our children to wrath but raise them up in the instruction of the Lord.

No matter the age, communication between parents and children must be treated the same way as you would in part as if communicating with an adult. I say in part, as you must show love, trust, honesty, and respect.

Too often as parents we tend to lie to children.

This is never a good practice. They quickly learn this habit, and trust me when I tell you, children pick up on when you are lying very quickly and easily.

What is important is to always have family time and what better time than at meal times. Make it a priority to have meals together as a family. The table is a great place for family discussion and finding out the daily happenings in each others' lives.

Always be open with your children. I learnt very quickly as a parent; I can't hide anything from my child. They will hear it on the outside.

Whatever you want them to learn, teach them. Don't leave it entirely up to their schoolteachers. It's your responsibility as parent/parents.

Teach your children about the Lord, pray with them in the mornings before school and at nights before bedtime.
Spend quality time with your children. Bond with them. Have separate bonding moments.
Let them spend quality time with father and mother separately as, sometimes what they can share with daddy, they may not share with mummy and vice versa.
Whatever is discussed, please let it be confidential.
As parents you can discuss, but let it stay between you both without any evidence that it was shared.

Another important note, please do not ill speak the other parent to the child/children. That's a bad practice and it causes dysfunction, lack of trust, discord and disrespect towards the other parent. Eventually they will resent you for ill speaking their other parent, especially when they realize it was only to build yourself up and show the other parent in a bad light.
When children are grown, please do not discuss what one child says to another.
You are actually building mistrust, as the other child will tell that child what you said.
I had four sisters and when either of us spoke to our mother and she discussed with another sister, we knew. Eventually we learned not to discuss certain things with her.

Always make sure you have family time together, take vacations together.
Have family game nights.

Do not have nannies and babysitters be an integral part of their lives.

Nannies and babysitters cannot be avoided, but they are not the primary teachers in their lives you are.

Children will always look up to their parents, you are their heroes.

They look to you for their security, for love, for food, for nurturing, support, and comfort.

Never put them down or make derogatory remarks.

Never tell them that they are not smart.

All children are born with their own gifts and talents.

It's up to you as the parents to discover and nurture that talent to its maximum potential.

Your children are individuals, you cannot force them to like and be pushed into what you like.

Too many parents want to live vicariously through their children. They want their children to be what they wanted to be, learn and study what as a parent you believe they should. Know your children's capabilities.

Educating your children is important and you should make sure they receive that education.

Talk to them, discover their passion and nurture it. Guide them through it.

Most children start off wanting to be a truck driver, or a fireman, until they reach the age of decision and then decide what they really want to be.

Be their biggest cheerleader. Talk to them about their dreams and aspirations.

Give them the support even if it is not what you want for them or where you see them.

This is where you quietly go into your prayer closet and pray for God to guide them.

MOST IMPORTANT: NEVER compare them to other children! Stop comparing them to other children in the family, your friends' children.
They are yours and are different. Each child has his or her gift and they have their own path and journey to walk. Their destiny was already mapped out by God.
You cannot expect them to comfortably walk in a size 9 shoe when their feet are size 3.

Always speak positive things over their lives. Talk to them in a positive attitude.
Encourage them, focus on their strengths.
Reward them for their accomplishments. If they do not achieve that passing grade, ask them how can you help them? Let them know it is not the end of the world and reassure them that with more focus they will do better the next report.
Do not chastise them for failing grades. Get the extra help needed, speak with their teachers to know how you can assist in improving their grades.

Prayer for Communication
with my children

Dear Lord, I thank you for blessing us with our child/children.
Your word says that they are a gift from You.
Help us as parents to treasure them as the gifts that they are.
Give us the wisdom on how to nurture them, Lord you are
our source and provider, help us to also provide for them
spiritually, physically, and emotionally.
Teach us to be great mentors to them. Just as You love us,
help us to love them and guide them to You.
Protect them Lord, give them wisdom.
Lord you said let the children be taught by You so that great
shall be their peace, so teach them Lord.
Let their tongues speak kindness and love to others.
Teach them Lord to be great listeners.
Help us as parents to communicate with them in love, mutual
respect, and trust.
Give them knowledge, understanding and wisdom in all
Literature and skill.
Give them the tongue of the learned and hands as pens of
ready writers.

Help us as parents to teach them and train them in the way You want us to Lord.

This we ask in Jesus' mighty name.

AMEN

Finances

Malachi 3:10-11

Bring all your tithes into the storehouse,
That there may be food in My house,
And try Me now in this,
"If I will not open for you the windows of heaven and pour out such a blessing
That there will not be room enough to receive it.
And I will rebuke the devourer for your sakes,
So that he will not destroy the fruit of your ground,
Nor shall the vine fail to bear fruit for you in the field.

Luke 6:38

Give and it shall be given to you; good measure, pressed down, shaken together, and running over will be put into your bosom.

Challenges in Life:
FINANCES

There comes a time in life we all go through a season when there is absolutely nothing!
This can be through a job loss; a divorce or migrating to another country, where you had to give up everything – family, friends, and job.

God knows what we need even before we have that need.
As a human being we look in all the places and people to fill that need before we go to God.
His plan is always for us to seek Him first! As **Matthew 6:33** tells us to Seek Ye first The Kingdom of Heaven, and ALL the rest will be added to you. Important is ALL not some, or a few but ALL!

I remember a time when I had no money, all I ate was popcorn & drank water for the better part of two years. My husband left and my son was away studying. It was a really tough time and I had to be there for my son emotionally and my phone bill was in a ridiculous way.
There was no way out of my financial crisis. Or so it seemed at that time.

My co-workers asked if I was in a perpetual fast as any time, they announced it was lunch time I would say no I am ok.

It was through that I decided or should I say the Holy Spirit moved me to fast and pray. I did just that. I fasted sometimes three days: seven days total water fast. It paid off.
I got stronger spiritually and emotionally. I started hearing God not always in an audible way but through my spirit.

I had to learn how to view finances through God's eyes. He outlines guidelines for money.
Most people tend to say Money is the root of all evil. That is not the word of God.
His word says in **1 Timothy 6:10**: The love of money is the root of all evil.
God also teaches us to Sow and to Reap; to feed the poor; to look after widows and orphans and most important How to Tithe.
Whenever God blesses us, IT IS NEVER FOR US ALONE! ALL blessings are to be shared.

I was born a catholic and I left Catholicism and became a Pentecostal Christian.
It was a time in my life I was searching for answers and help in the most challenging time of my life.
I never looked back. I found my peace, I discovered who I am, and it is on that continuous journey that my life with God is a work in progress. Do I stumble yes, but He promised in **Colossians 2: 6-7** If I stumble, I will not fall, because The Lord holds my hand.

Challenges – Finances

Sowing & Reaping

2 Corinthians 9:6-7

Whoever sows sparingly will also reap sparingly, and whoever sows generously will also reap generously.
Give what is in your heart, not grudgingly, for God loves a cheerful giver.

Challenges – Finances

My first lesson or should I say test that God put to me (I smile as I remembered that struggle).

I was standing in service and one day the Lord asked me to give eight hundred dollars.

I cringed and looked around as if "You not talking to me!"

I heard it again. I grudgingly took out my cheque book and wrote out the cheque and give it.

I then repented as I heard: God loves a cheerful giver.

The next day I went to work, the accountant called me and asked me to come to the office.

Guess what! They claimed that they short paid me $2400 plus dollars and handed me the cheque!

After that I began sowing and it was indeed a joy to sow seeds.

I did not care about the harvest. I just started to sow into various areas of ministry (Dorcas).

Areas that I made sure to sow was Back to School, Thanksgiving and Christmas. Those are exceedingly difficult times for many who are less fortunate.

This is not something I go boasting about as He spoke about helping without the fanfare as **Matthew 6:2** says when you give to the needy you do not announce it.

It is a humbling experience, and some people are embarrassed to ask for help.

2 Corinthians 9:6 says when you sow sparingly, you will reap sparingly. If you sow generously, you will reap generously.

People say give until it hurts. I hate hearing that! It must never hurt to give.

God will always rest it on your heart where to sow your seed. Because He wants you to reap a bountiful harvest. If you are not sure ask Him, He will tell you

Challenge of Life: Finances

Tithes:

Proverbs 3:9-10
Honor the Lord with your wealth, with the first fruits of your crops.
Then your barns will be filled to overflowing, and your vats will brim over with new wine.

Leviticus 27:30
A tithe from the land, whether grain from the soil or fruit from the trees, belongs to the Lord.

Tithes

Tithes represent 10% of your income that is given to the church where you fellowship.

Tithing was my biggest and hardest hurdle to even understand. It took a lot of reading of the word, praying and understanding that the Lord promised that He will always take care of His people, if we are faithful and obedient.

Obedience is the key factor if we want to receive from God. There are many scriptures about tithing in the bible, but my favorite two are **Malachi 3:10** which He challenges us to bring all our tithes into the storehouse, so that there may be food in His house.

This means that the ministry gets the tithes so that the ministry can continue feeding the sheep which is us.

He even went as far as to ask us to test Him and see that He will not open the windows of heaven, that He will pour out a blessing that we won't have room for it! And if that was not enough, He even promised to rebuke the devourer of our harvest.

The second scripture is **Luke 6:38** – Give and it will be given to you, full measure, pressed down, shaken and running over.

That is the guarantee we have from God that He is our provider if we are faithful and obedient in our finances.

All He asks for is the one tenth of our earnings. If we read His Word from the Old Testament to the new it spoke about the importance of Tithing. Even though we come under grace in the New Testament, that now means that we do not do the burnt offerings as they did in the Old Testament.

We often spend more than the one tenth on trivial and inconsequential things.

When we first honor God, He makes sure that lack; poverty; not enough and the devourer of our harvest does not attack our finances.

Tithing guarantees that He will always provide for us.

Offerings: this is what we put weekly when we attend church services. This is in addition to the tithes.

Then we have first fruits which is one tenth of money I receive. Example anytime I get a gift of money, I always make sure that I take the one tenth and put it into the basket.

Your finances and how you spend, as a married couple should always be discussed with each other.

Be obedient to God's requirements for finances and all will be well. Whether as a couple or single, the same rule/principle applies.

Challenges of Life: Finances

Giving & Offerings:
It is always easier to give when we know that we are getting something in return.

When we give, we must always give freely, expecting nothing in return.

Giving is a heart matter. There are some people who have that spirit, a spirit of giving.

When they give you literally see their eyes are lit with joy.

In **Matthew 6:2**, God warns us about giving and (in my words) putting it on a microphone!

This means that we should not make a public announcement of what we give.

Too many people do this.

Giving should be done with no strings attached or with any conditions. Then it is not giving, it's a loan.

Tithes belong to God. Tithes are used to build the ministry and to take care of the Shepherd and the flock.

Tithes are given when you receive your salary, you take out the one tenth and give to the ministry where you fellowship.

Offerings are gifts that are given to express thanks. We do this weekly when we attend church.

Giving is a part of life.

You give of yourself, you give of your time, you give in a tangible way.

When we honor God with our giving, He promises to give us full measure. **Luke 6:38**

That is not to say that is the reason we give. Because He also says that He loves a cheerful giver. **2 Corinthians 9:7**

When we hoard and act miserly, He views this as we are servants to money in other words, money becomes our God.

Ecclesiastes 5:13 tells us that wealth hoarded does so to the harm of the owner.

Proverbs 28:22 says a miserly man hastens after wealth and does not know that poverty will come upon him.

If we trust in the Lord and see Him as our Source and Provider, no good thing will He withhold from us.

Psalm 23:1 says, The Lord is my Shepherd, I shall not want.

Prayer over Finances

Heavenly Father I come to You with praise and thanksgiving for who You are and for being my provider.

I thank You for Your hand of provision not only in finances but in my kneading bowls and baskets, my job, and my business. May my pantry never lack. As I rebuke poverty, lack and just enough. May there always be surplus and replenishment. May I always have to give.

I declare over my life that I will be a lender always never a borrower. I declare that you will prosper the work of my hands and everything that I undertake to do, as I honor You with the work of my hands.

Help me to be a good steward over my finances. I declare Lord, You are first in my life and it's You that I serve, not money or things.

Help me to be trustworthy over what I already have.

Help me to remember the less fortunate and to extend my hands towards them where I can.

Keep me humble in my harvest.

Lord make me a blessing.

In Jesus' name I pray,
Amen.

Peace

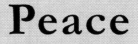

Phillipians 4:6-7
Do not be anxious for anything, but in every situation, by prayer
and petition, with thanksgiving,
Present your requests to God, and the peace of God, which
transcends all understanding,
Will guard your hearts and your minds in Christ Jesus.

Matthew 5:9
Blessed are the peacemakers, for they shall be called children
of God.

Challenge of Life: Peace

In life, peace is difficult to achieve. Our life as we know it, is always filled and busy, especially if children are involved. We long to have peace and quiet. Peace of mind.
What exactly do we mean by Peace? Peace means serenity, quiet, rest.
Peace comes from the assurance that I am safe, I have financial and emotional security. My home is harmonious.

How can we achieve this peace?
By trusting and focusing on the Lord. He says to be anxious for nothing but in everything by prayer and supplication with thanksgiving.
Peace within oneself – Maintaining your peace whether at work or home can be challenging. The phone is either always ringing, or there is always something to do, where we could never sit and breathe in and just have a moment to ourselves.
When we want that peace and quiet, then the last thing we should be doing is watching movies that are loaded with action or anything that makes us anxious.
Some friends also are so filled with drama that after talking to them you feel your head just entered a whirlwind, or sometimes they just sucked out all your energy. This is when we need to avoid those friends and instead of watching a

movie, just sit out in the garden with a cup of tea or just take a quiet walk and enjoy nature.
Do things that will contribute to your peace.

Peace is a fruit of the Holy Spirit, and one should always try to get that inner peace.
It is hard to maintain peace especially in the midst of trials and storms.
When we learn to trust and have utmost faith in the Lord this is when we have inner peace.
Phillipians 4:7 says that the peace of God which surpasses every understanding, will guard our hearts and minds.
A peace of mind is so important to have. And God promises us that peace.
Isaiah 26:3 says that if we keep focused on and trust the Lord that peace of mind is guaranteed.

It is human nature for us to worry, we worry about bills, children, jobs, friends, but if only we place our trust in the Lord, we should not have to worry.
Have you ever come across someone who is always smiling and always very soft spoken and wonder how they are like that? That is the peace of God in them.
They may be going through a battle, but they will always say God is love and He will see me through.
They even radiate that peace. It is like nothing phases them.
As we say do not sweat the small stuff.

Trusting that the Lord has us reminds me of **Matthew 8:24** when there was a storm and Jesus was asleep during the storm and the disciples were struggling. Now that is the peace we must strive for!

A couple of people that I constantly read about in the bible that had peace, because they knew that God had their backs were:

Daniel, when he was thrown into the lion's den; Joseph a perfect example who held onto the dream that God gave him. He kept his peace through his trials and tribulations.

Prayer for peace

Heavenly Father you are peace, you promised me that if I stay focused on You that you will give me the peace that surpasses every understanding.

Father may I always trust You, that even in my storms and trying times, in tribulation, that I can find that peace.

May I always know You, the author and finisher of my life.

I pray that my mind will be staid on You so that I can have perfect peace.

Help me to be anxious for nothing. Remove all my fears and doubts so that I can enjoy peace.

It is through faith that I have peace with You.

Let peace rule in my heart, let there be peace in my home at my office.

Your peace Lord is all I need with thanks and praise.

In Jesus's mighty name I pray,

Amen.

Patience

Proverbs 15:18
Hot tempers cause arguments;
But patience brings peace.

Romans 12:12
Rejoice in hope, be patient in tribulation,
Be constant in prayer.

Challenges of Life: Patience

Patience. As we say never pray for Patience! You will find yourself in many a trial and tribulation for that to be perfected in your life!
Patience is when we endure adversity without complaining, when we hold steadfast to God in the middle of the storms, endurance of the current challenges in your life.

In my days of adversity, and those days must come because they are there to strengthen our faith and trust in God. It took a great deal of staying silent and not answering back. Many a time I had to pray for God to let my tongue cleave to the roof of my mouth. Because a harsh answer will certainly open the door to anger and strife.
In anger we must exercise caution as what we say in anger can never be retracted and the hurt and damage has already been done.
Even if we apologize to the hurt person, the words will remain in that person's spirit, and it would hurt the relationship.

Patience is required in our relationships, especially with our spouses.

We are not all perfect and sometimes we have to overlook minor things that they do. Like, leaving the utensils in the sink, eating, and dropping crumbs on the carpet and chairs. Minor things. It is not worth getting angry and get to boiling point.

Yes, I agree that you can discuss it, but ponder first, if to nag about it and open the door to strife is worth it.

Proverbs 25:24 says It is better to live in the corner of the roof than to live with a nagging wife.

Remember love is always patient (1 Corinthians 13:4). Love keeps no record of wrongdoings.

A constant nagging spouse, who continuously points out wrongdoing and faults, contributes as a form of abuse.

Proverbs 15:1 says a soft answer turns away wrath.

How we treat with adversity can either break us or take us to another level in Christ.

Do you ever notice that in the middle of our trials the devil is more active? Oh yes. He sends his minions to laugh at us, heap the negative words in our spirit, torture, and torment us in our thoughts and minds and if we are not careful it can send us into depression, where we cannot even pray.

To develop patience, which is a fruit of the Holy Spirit, it takes time. Even years to develop. If we are not patient in the little things, we will not have patience in the major storms. Patience means perseverance. Perseverance means to suffer long. But **Hebrews 10:35-36** tells us to be steadfast in God. We must hold onto our faith in Him.

Remember that God operates in His timetable not ours.

How do we develop patience? James 1:2-4 tells us it is in testing or the harsh challenges in life that tries our faith, the tribulations develop our patience.

In trials and tribulations, this is when we should lock in with God, have a small core support prayer group. Try to stay in the word and ask God to give you Grace and strength to persevere, for our troubles were not meant to be punishment, but as training.

Patience is a virtue; some liken patience with Job.

I always pondered why the saying "you have the patience of Job"

But in reading about Job, he had strength. I felt a sense that he was always in a pensive mode. Listening to his friends and wife that were all naysayers. But not having much to say or when he spoke it was always hopeful or at times, he felt like he deserved what was happening to him. That was quiet patience if you asked me.

Nevertheless, until you have strong faith, having patience is hard.

Prayer for Patience

Heavenly Father, I thank you that even in the midst of my trials and tribulations I still have You.

I can hold fast unto You. Help me Lord to understand that the trying and testing is to build patience.

Help me Lord to always have a soft answer and the right intonation in speaking with others.

Lord there are times when I am tired but help me to remember that it is in my weakness, You are made strong.

Help me to hold on to my faith and trust in You so that I shall see my reward.

Help me to always remember that the race is not for the swiftest, but for those who can endure.

Give me the strength and the grace to persevere to the end.

Help me to be patient in tribulation and constantly stay in prayer and in Your presence.

Lord, I give You all the Thanks, all the honor and all the Glory in Jesus' mighty name,

AMEN.

Faithfulness

Ephesians 5:25

Husbands love your wives, just as Christ loves the church and gave for her.

Proverbs 19:21

Many are the plans of a man's heart, but it is the Lord's purpose that prevails.

We are to be faithful to God because He is faithful to us.

Challenges in Life: Faithfulness

Faithfulness is an extremely broad term. If we take this in reference to marriage it means just that. Being faithful to your spouse.

Too many times there is unfaithfulness in marriages. A spouse run at the slightest sign of trouble.

The Grass IS NOT GREENER on the other side people!!!

The marriage bed is to be undefiled! What do I mean? It must be kept pure; it is ONLY for the intimacy between a husband and a wife.

God will judge adulterers. The one thing I do know from firsthand experience is that the judgement that falls on a cheating spouse is very harsh.

They go through a stripping; the adulteress eventually leaves as the relationship never lasts.

The spouse becomes resentful to the adulteress. There will always be strife between the two.

It is always up to the other spouse whether they want you back or they move forward without reconciliation.

It is God to give you the Grace to be able to take that spouse back and forgive without ever bringing up that incident in an argument. Or even talking about it. It takes God and therapy to put that marriage back with healing of both parties. Both need to understand why it happened in the first place.

Faithfulness is also about the character of a person. Can I rely on that person? Is that person loyal, dependable, and consistent.

Am I faithful to God?
For us to receive blessings from God, we must be faithful to Him, and His word. He must see that He can trust us. For He says in **Luke 16:10**, He that is faithful in that which is least, is faithful also in much. The same can be said that those that are unfaithful in the least cannot be trusted in much.
God expects me to be faithful to Him in the good times as well as the tough times.
Can God depend on me? Just as we can ask: Can I depend on my spouse in the good times and bad?
God is always faithful to us, even when we fail Him. It is just who He is. He loves us even in our mess.

Prayer for faithfulness

Heavenly Father, You, who are faithful to us, even in our faithlessness. Help us to trust You more.

Help us Lord to be faithful to You always. Strengthen and sustain through trials, that we remain steadfast knowing that You will deliver us.

Lord we commit our works unto You so that our thoughts shall be established.

Keep us from temptations of the flesh Lord, may we die to self, Lord, kill all our fleshly desires and what is not of You that's present in us.

Lord, we thank You that you are faithful to us, that You are steadfast in your love for us. Knowing that Lord, comforts us. May we remain faithful to you.

Keep our feet on the paths of righteousness for Your name's sake.

We pray that You will always give light for the step we are on, in Jesus' mighty name,

AMEN.

Self-Control

Proverbs 25:28
He that has no rule over his spirit, is like a city broken down and without walls.

James 1:14-15
Each one is tempted when he is drawn away by his own desires and enticed.
When the desires are conceived, it gives birth to sin, and when sin is full-grown,
It brings forth death.

Challenges of Life: Self Control

This is another broad area to be discussed.
When we do not have self-control, we will be slaves to what controls us.
It can be Food, Lust, Money, our Behavior.
Having no self-control can only result in grave consequences in the many areas of our lives.
Self-Control is the ability to respond and behave correctly.
It is not giving into our canal nature or fleshly desires.
Lacking self-control is a total lack of discipline.

Self-control in our behavior.

Do you know anyone whether it is a family member, friend, or spouse that at the drop of a hat when there is a conversation and it hits the nerve of that person, suddenly they get up and push back the chair and their voice rises and is above everyone else's?
Even at the most trivial matter, they are so thin-skinned, the temper rises.
That is a person that lacks self-control. They are cantankerous.

Even if there is a discussion or a conversation at hand, we cannot always agree, it's human nature that we are all different and see-through different lenses or have different perspectives and opinions on various matters. But is not healthy to be flying off at everyone when we disagree, or the topic hits a nerve.

Some conversations can get heated and go from zero to a hundred in the blink of an eye.

We can agree to disagree. Even if the remarks made were derogatory to us, self-control is walking away peacefully, we do not have to be all happy and smile but try to leave in a calm manner.

People who lack self-control need prayers. They carry an angry spirit, a spirit of strife, and it could be something from in their past.

Proverbs 29:11 tells us that A fool always loses his temper. But a wise man holds it back.

Even if we are angry about something someone said and trust me some people can be very insensitive towards others, we can quietly ask the Lord to "set a watch over my mouth and keep the door of my lips. (**Psalm 141:3-4**)

Normally I ask the Lord to let my tongue cleave to the roof of my mouth. (**Psalm 137:6**).

Even if I feel that I must answer because sometimes you do, but try to answer when the situation is calm, if at that point in time it is volatile, then walk away and probably discuss later through a phone call but ask that the Holy Spirit speak through you to that person.

Answering back in the heat of the moment always ends with hurtful words that we cannot take back! That can cause permanent hurt to both parties.

Self-Control and Lust

Being lustful is a sin of the flesh.

Most times lust leads to adultery and fornication. This destroys a marriage.

God speaks about this very strongly and adultery is one of the commandments that He asks us to not commit.

Matthew 5:28 puts it very bluntly: when you look at a woman with lustful intent, you have already committed adultery! That is speaking to the married man. Yes, it goes to you also, the wife.

The only way we can avoid this behavior and stay away from things of the world is by staying in the word and asking God to take away all our fleshly desires.

We should always walk in the spirit and not in the flesh.

This can only be developed by practicing what the word tells us.

We should never allow impulsive behavior to get the better of us.

Marriage must be honorable, and the marriage bed be undefiled and kept pure.

Contributors to this behavior are alcohol that leads to drunken behavior, looking at pornography, wild parties, lewd behavior, and partying.

These are what a man and woman of God should not partake in.

It will not only destroy your marriage, if there are children involved, those children will go through the trauma of parents divorcing, the upheaval of the home and the security of having both parents and the safety and wellbeing of the children.

This impacts their lives well into their adulthood.

Too many people are walking around today with the scars of broken homes.

This is where generational curses and curse spirits of inheritance come in.

Why is Self-Control Important?

Self-Control protects us, we are better people when we exercise self-control.
Will there be trials and temptations? A resounding YES!
Self-Control can be hard and frustrating. Trust me it is awfully hard to stay quiet when all you want is to blow someone's head off or cuss them out.
We must expect the trials and temptations, but thankfully we do not have to do it alone, we have the help of The Holy Spirit who will help us to overcome all temptation.

Self-control protects us from getting into trouble in reference to lustful behavior.
The devil is always roaming to see who he can devour. Let it not be you!

A person that has self-control is not easily distracted by outside "noise."
They fill their time usefully and are more focused on achieving their goals, which results in success.

There will always be that "friend" who will pop in and try to take you from home, to go to have a drink in a bar, go watch a game, visit other friends and a million other things.

You leave your wife and children at home, and you would have spent the afternoon and well into the night and into the wee hours of the morning before you return home.

That is the main ingredient for strife, discord, and quarrel in the home.

That is not the friend that you should have around you and your family.

Self-control is putting your family first.

Always make sure that your priorities are in order.

Prayer for Self-Control

Heavenly Father when the world is so out of control, help us to retain self-control.
Help us Lord to add goodness, and to goodness, knowledge and to knowledge, self-control.
Help us to be slow to speak and slow to anger.
Help us always to say no to ungodliness and worldly passions.
Lord help us to live with self-control and uprightly.
Help us not to turn to the right or to the left, Lord, keep our feet from all evil.
Help us always to listen to hear Your voice and only Your voice and be obedient to You and Your word.
Lord we pray that we will be always sober-minded, vigilant and use good judgement in all things.
AMEN.

Joy

Nehemiah 8:10
The joy of the Lord is your strength.

Romans 15:13
May the God of hope fill you with joy and peace in believing….

Challenges in Life: JOY

To have Joy is to be in a state of happiness and gladness. Our hearts sing when we are in a joyful mood. The people around us are affected by our joy as it is transferable.
All the things that bring joy to our hearts: Birth of a baby; a new home; family fun; a day at the beach; a beautiful drive. So many things give us that joyous, elated feeling.
Some seasons bring joy to us – Christmas; Thanksgiving, any special holiday brings joy.

What can take away our Joy? Anything that is negative. Gossip; Constant Complaining and nagging, quarreling in the home; discord; strife and the two that stands out as important is bad circumstances and Prayerlessness.

When a home has no joy it's impossible to stay and live in it. The atmosphere is filled with oppression and depression. There is a deathly silence as we walk on eggshells because someone is angry. The atmosphere is thick and there is a dark cloud hanging.

A home filled with the Holy Spirit and prayer will always be light, filled with peace and joy.

There is laughter and a light atmosphere in the house.
We should always try to make our home our sanctuary, a place where we can find rest, relaxation, peace, and comfort. Our homes should be free from all negativities.

When you see that the home is beginning to lose the laughter and the joy, sit and talk about what is happening and what are the issues that is causing the loss of joy.
It can be a financial crisis, a loss of a job, loss of a family member, whatever it is, discuss and have dialogue about it. There is always a solution. Bring prayer and fasting into the equation.
If there is a job loss, then the solution will be to sit together as a family and discuss where the reduction in expenses can be. But always try to solve the problem together. Never shoulder the burden on your own.
Pray that God who is our source and provider of your home open another door.
It is only for a season but keeping your joy during this trial, will shorten the season, as God looks to us for a right response.

Prayer for a Joyful Heart

Heavenly Father, who is the source of our Joy, may we always look to You as the author and finisher of our lives.
You said in Your word Lord that we should always have joyful hearts.
Lord, you said that we ought to rejoice always and give thanks in all circumstances. Whatever we must face today, good, or bad, help us to rely on You the source of everything. Help us to delight ourselves in You. Give us the garments of praise for the feelings of heaviness.
Help me to come to you always with joy, so that in Your presence, in Your company we will be refreshed.

This we ask in Jesus' name.

AMEN

Long-Suffering

Ephesians 4:2
With all lowliness and meekness, with longsuffering, fore bearing one another in love.

Colossians 1:11
Strengthened with all might, according to His glorious power, unto all patience and longsuffering with joyfulness.

Challenges in Long-Suffering

What does Long-Suffering really mean?
Long-Suffering means to patiently endure hardship.

Have you ever felt that as you start to enjoy a certain level of serenity, peace and joy, something comes to upset that period of rest?
It's as if you can never have a long season of rest.

Sometimes I think about David, who in his wilderness season wrote 75 Psalms!
These Psalms that he wrote were filled with every emotion.
Emotions of Love, adoration, peace, joy, emotions of sadness, crying, anger and it also showed us the longsuffering he went through.
But as **James 1:2-4** says: Count it all joy when we face trials of many kinds.

David's suffering was long in that he was fleeing from his son Absalom and then from king Saul.
From biblical account David spent thirteen (13) years running and hiding from king Saul.

In reading the psalms you can see that the most beautiful psalms were written in his longsuffering. This led me to understand that even in the midst of his longsuffering, trials and tribulations, he was still able to trust in the Lord and find peace, comfort and joy.

Did he cry, YES! Did he get angry? YES! Psalm 4:4 was where he instructed us that we can get angry, but sin not. He also tells us that in anger we should stay silent and ponder and reflect what is in our hearts and why the anger is there.

Sometimes what we are angry about is not really the root cause.

Oftentimes we take our anger out on the wrong person and cover the real issue with something else.

How many times in our longsuffering we question God, we lose hope, we lose patience and yes, we even get angry with God. Well at least I have at times gotten angry, to the point I start to believe that God does not love me that's why I am suffering and maybe I am not worthy, or I don't deserve anything good.

It's times and seasons of long-suffering, that I must go into a period of fasting and seek God's face for His strength, to seek what needs to be changed in my life. What is He trying to tell me?

Spend more time in His word. It's a struggle to praise and worship even though this is what is the best way to go through the longsuffering.

Someone once told me that the problem is never with God, it's always with us.

It's something God wants to change in us. He wants a certain response.

He is teaching us through the longsuffering.

We must remember He suffered also, but He took it with great patience, great compassion, and great love.

There are so many biblical stories of people who went through longsuffering and how they managed to overcome the longsuffering and still trust, still worship, still have hope and still stayed in God's peace and presence.

Joseph who was betrayed by his own brothers suffered long. But he held on to the dream God gave him. Joseph's pit into the palace experience lasted thirteen years. Just like David, he held on to the promises of God. Joseph was very patient throughout his longsuffering. It's what we do in the time of our suffering and how quickly we learn the lessons, is what would in part, dictate the length of season.

Depending on the destiny that God has mapped for us and His plan for our lives, is how long He will keep us in longsuffering.

Prayer in Longsuffering

Heavenly Father, I thank You for loving me, for watching over me, for Your angels that are encamped around me.

Lord, it is through great trials and longsuffering, that You draw us closer to You.

You have my destiny in the palm of Your hands.

I can't always see what you are doing, but where I can't trace Your hand, help me to always trust Your heart.

Strengthen and sustain me through my pit experience. It is in my weakness You are made strong.

Help me to count it all joy that my longsuffering will not be in vain, but for Your greater glory. That this is the way You have mapped out for my life, so that when I come before the seat of judgement, I can stand and hear You say: "Well done, good and faithful servant".

Thank You Lord that through this my faith is strengthened and that I will always honor and serve You.

AMEN.

Kindness

Ephesians 4:32
Be kind and compassionate to one another, forgiving each other, just as Christ forgave you.

Proverbs 31:26
She opens her mouth with wisdom, and kindness is on her tongue.

Challenges of life: Kindness

Kindness is the quality of a person who is friendly, generous, respectful, and considerate.

Not everyone has the personality to be compassionate and selfless.
All of us at some point exhibit selfishness and have been inconsiderate to others' feelings.

When we look at the life of Jesus, we know that He showed great compassion. His mercies are new every day.
People that lack a moral compass also lack that spirit of kindness.

In speaking with a friend recently, she remarked that her experience is that sometimes, it's her own family that lacked kindness.
She remarked that sometimes it's the act of selfishness and the disrespect that was hard for her to continuously accommodate them in her home.

I indicated to her, sometimes you must pray for them as even in our saved selves, the devil can use the best of us to irritate another.

Even in the church, there are some who can't show the act of kindness.

Have you ever noticed that sometimes, it's when we are in our worst days, when we need that kindness that it's nowhere to be found?

It's important that no matter where we are, we must always be kind to others.

You will never know with some people that they are in crisis and that's the moment we need to be kind to them. It can change their day. It can even give them that extra encouragement to continue their journey. It's through that one act of kindness, that we may have stopped them from going over the edge. Kindness can renew hope in them.

Kindness costs nothing.

The bible says that we must always be kind and compassionate.

Sometimes through our own selfishness, we are only concerned about ourselves, what we are going through, what we need and totally forget that there is a family member or a friend that need our compassion.

Kindness and compassion should be part of our nature.

If we have a selfish nature, you will see that kindness and compassion is not resident.

The two can't co-exist.

If we read **1 Corinthians 13:4**; you will see that love is patient and kind.

Be kind without expectations.

Prayer for Kindness

Heavenly Father, I thank you for teaching me that You are the epitome of what love and kindness is.

Teach me your ways Lord.

Help me to always remember that kindness and compassion is who You are and that if I walk in the Spirit, then that is who I should always be.

Fill me Lord with a compassionate heart. Let my heart and hand be stretched out in kindness.

Kill the selfish part of me that would hinder me from being kind.

Let me speak kind words and give me a compassionate heart Lord.

Let me always show respect and empathy towards others, in Jesus' name.

AMEN

Goodness

2 Peter 1:5
Make every effort to add to your faith Goodness and to goodness, knowledge…

Romans 8:28
We know that all things work together for good to them that love God, to them that are called according to His purpose.

Challenges of Life: Goodness

There is a difference between Kindness and Goodness. In writing, I thought about merging the two, because I thought that they were both and the same. That is, until I researched the meanings of both.

Kindness involves being generous and considerate. Being unselfish.

Goodness is about doing what is right. Being pure and righteous. Goodness in essence is Godliness.

For me, goodness is love in action!

We often hear about the goodness of God. There are thousands of testimonies about the goodness of God that we read and hear about.

The anniversary of 9/11 was just remembered, and the goodness of God was heard when people who were supposed to be in those buildings and through the goodness of God, they either stayed at home or were late that day and are alive today.

We also hear all the time and even say it that "God is Good". Especially when a crisis was avoided.

God is good says that it is not just what He does, but who He is.

As **Psalm 46:1** says, He is our refuge and strength, a present help in time of trouble, that is why we should have that confidence in Him to know that He is good.

Do you know that there are some people who can't receive goodness?

Oh yes!

These are the people who have been hurt, people who has never experienced love in their lives. When you are good to them, they believe that you want something from them.

How can we demonstrate goodness?

Give a needed hug, a listening ear over a cup of tea, a phone call, make their favorite dish. This is called: Goodness is love in action!

A scripture verse we hear all the time and know it is from Psalm 23:6 Surely goodness and mercy shall follow me...

We can't show goodness if our hearts are not right.

Goodness emulated from a person is the character of that person. You can't fake goodness. Goodness is given through the Grace of God.

Goodness is a fruit of the Holy Spirit and God wants us to grow in the fruits of the Spirit, so that our lives can be filled with love.

Prayer for Goodness

Lord, I come to You, praying that I be made whole. Where there is anything present in my life that does not represent you, remove it.

Lord, You said that if a branch does not bear fruit, you cut it off. Cut every branch that does not bear fruit, Lord, prune the dead areas of my life.

Help me to be an example of who You are.

Lord, may I always be pure of heart so that I can show goodness and kindness to everyone I meet.

Just as Your goodness and mercy follow me, Lord let me represent goodness to others.

Let me always be kind and compassionate, and just as You listen to me, let my ears be attentive to others also.

This I ask in Jesus' name.

AMEN

Gentleness

1 Thessalonians 2:7
But we are gentle among you, like a nursing mother taking care of her own children.

2 Samuel 22:36
You have given me your shield of salvation, and your gentleness made me great

Challenges of Life: Gentleness

Gentleness is showing care and respect for others.
Gentleness is important to God as it also carries a personality of humility and being meek.
Gentleness sounds like softness.
Soft words, kind words, moving in humility.

Have you ever come across some people that are crass, rough, loud voices, don't care what they say or how they say it?
As we have always heard the phrase: "It's not what you say, but how you say it".
Then there are some people who can't help that they have that loud booming voice, and are rough, but they mean well? They are like those huge teddy bears that have a great heart and always mean well it's just that they are a bit rough around the edges. They are still the lovable people. They are also humble.

In some marriages, there is no gentleness. Some husbands and wives don't know how to demonstrate gentleness, and this may happen because they grew up in a home where there was always violence, people speaking to each other in a rough manner.

There was no love, or love was shown in a rough way. Manners were not part of the teachings in that home.

Always remember that a soft answer turns away wrath, but a harsh answer stirs up anger. **Proverbs 15:1**

How can we change and become gentle? This is an act that we must practice every day until it becomes a part of our character.

Some believe that to be gentle is to be weak. Far from the truth!

Gentleness is a show of strength. We sometimes think that strength should be demonstrated by aggression and violence. That's what the world wants us to believe.

But true strength comes from gentleness, a fine character trait to possess.

Gentleness is a feeling of calm, peace, and softness. Gentleness is a behavior that is shown even when things are not going right.

A person who lacks gentleness is easily angered and is often vengeful.

Andy Mort explains that "gentleness is not reactionary. People who show gentleness are those that have self-control".

A person that shows gentleness reflects humility and does not act in haste.

Lauren Abraham says in her devotional that "gentleness comes from having a love for others".

For us to develop a spirit of gentleness, we must first acknowledge that gentleness is a strength not a weakness. See that God even in our sinfulness, He remains gentle towards us, and we should also do the same.

It is in having loving hearts that gentleness is manifested. When our children are hurt through falls, they expect us to be gentle in administering medication.

So too when we as adults are hurting we expect others to be gentle with us through our pain.

Prayer for Gentleness

Dear Lord,
Teach me how to be gentle in spirit.
I can't be gentle until I learn humility, softness and be at peace.
Humble my human spirit, let the words that come from my mouth be pleasing to You.
Let my intonation be soft towards others. Even when they make me angry Lord, help me to show kindness, love, compassion and let my answer be soft and gentle.

Let me not be reactive to when others hurt me but help me to be understanding of others.
Let my words be always kind and loving.

Thank You Lord for the work You are doing in me.

AMEN

Friends

John 15:13

Greater love than has no one than this: to lay down one's life for one's friends.

Proverbs 18:24

One who has unreliable friends soon comes to ruin, but there is a friend that sticks closer than a brother.

Challenges in Life....
FRIENDS

In life friends are so important.

What is a friend? Webster defines the meaning as "A person who has a strong liking for and trust in another; a person that helps and supports, a person you are fond of, with whom you spend time with and with whom you talk.

What does the bible say about what a friend is? In **John 15:13** Jesus puts it so aptly – Greater love has no one than this, that he lay down his life for his friends.

What a friend we have in Jesus as He laid His life down for us. One of the best examples of friendship was the bond between David and Jonathan (King Saul's son). Despite his father wanting to kill David, Jonathan stood by David.

That friendship ran deep as we see **in 1 Samuel 18:1** – Jonathan's soul was knitted to David and Jonathan loved David as his own soul.

Jonathan and David made a covenant with each other, and Jonathan took off his robe and gave it to David.

In life it's very rare that we can have friends like Jonathan and David. Friends whom we can trust with everything. We can bare our souls to that person. That one friend who will stand with us through our problems, break ups, divorce, good times, friends that can celebrate with us births, baptisms, weddings, and birthdays.

It is just as challenging to keep and maintain these close bonds, as sometimes these friends can come into our lives for a season.
There are some friends that are fair weather friends, meaning that in the good times they are there, but in the challenging times they disappear.
These fair-weather friends we sometimes learn the hardest lessons as we trusted them with our secrets, but in our challenging times they are no where to be found and everything we trusted them with was exposed. There is a saying that when thieves fall out, it's a bad thing.

God sometimes place people in our lives to carry us through the various seasons of life.
Depending on what season we are in, we need strong faith filled friends who can help pray us through the challenging seasons, the trial and tribulation season.
There are times we also must go through our wilderness period without a friend. Just like David. In these times the only one we can turn to is Jesus.
Amos 3:3 gives us the insight into the importance of a friend – Can two walk together, except they be agreed.
Jesus when he sent out His disciples, He sent them out in twos. They were stronger in pairs.
Matthew 18:19 says that whenever two of us on earth agree about anything we pray for, it will be done for us by the Father in heaven. (As long as it is according to His will and done with the right motives). That right there is the power

of having a great friend with whom you can pray together for both your situations.

I remember I had this really great friend who became like a sister to me. Actually, I had two of those relationships. I never in my wildest dream thought that I would lose the friendship in part. I say in part as, with one we still keep in touch, but we are not as close as we used to be. The other just refused to take my calls and messages.

Hannah was like my sister, we went everywhere together, she was always at my home. When my husband and I broke up, I couldn't get the support I wanted spiritually from her. We both acknowledged it and she was hurting so badly for me, and it was because of her lack of spiritually, she admitted she couldn't be there for me as she felt helpless. I was devastated, but we still maintain a very cordial relationship from a distance. I was more understanding of why it had to be.

The second friend came in at the time Hannah was removed. Kats, as I call her, I believe was a friend God replaced Hannah with. Kats was a prayer warrior, and she has a great gift of discernment. She taught me so much, and that is an understatement! I came to rely on her for everything spiritual, we fasted and prayed together, she became my go to person to understand all my challenges in life. I relied on her. Little did I notice that she became my God. So instead of going to God I went to her.

I believe that's why God removed her from my life.

I have learnt in life do not be discouraged when friends are gone. Sometimes depending on the season in life we cannot always carry them. This was evident in the life of Abraham in **Genesis 12** when God told Abraham to leave his family and all that he knew and go to the land that He will show him. That could not have been easy. Abraham was seventy-five years and that is an extremely hard adjustment to have made at that age in life.

Abraham took his nephew, Lot, with him and we even see that a separation between them took place after awhile **Genesis 13:5.**

Friends are an important part of our lives, this is not to say that we would never have long term friends, but some are to last for a season. But to God be the Glory when we have lifelong friends.

It is important as a couple to have friends that can give us support and advice. It is important for our children to have the right friends in their lives. This is an important aspect that must be kept in prayer

Prayer for My Friends

Heavenly Father, we thank you for the gift of friends and friendships. Father your word says that greater love than no one has than to lay down one's life for his friends.
Lord, help me to be that friend. A friend that sticks closer than a brother.
Lord, I pray that you send the right friend into my life, my husband's life, my child/children's life.
Friends who would be what Aaron and Hun were to Moses in the day of battle.
Lord, help me to always be there for my friends in time of need. Whether it be in prayer or moral support.
Help me to always stretch my hand out in time of need, spiritually, emotionally, and physically.

May I always remember also what a friend I have in Jesus, who bear all my griefs all my pain and suffering. That even though I am in that valley of the shadows of death, I will fear no evil for thou art with me.

Lord, I thank you for my friends and pray that you protect our friendships, fill us with love and joy and peace in Jesus' name we pray.

AMEN

Forgiveness

Luke 17:3
If your brother sins against you, rebuke him and if he repents, forgive him.

Matthew 6:14
For if you forgive others when they sin against you, your heavenly Father will also forgive you.

Challenges of Life: Forgiveness

I could never write about anything, and Forgiveness would not be included.
Forgiveness is such an important key element in life.
For us to live a life free of condemnation, we must first forgive ourselves.
If we do not forgive ourselves, then we cannot forgive others.

Greater Good Berkeley says that psychologists define forgiveness as a decision to release feelings of resentment and vengeance towards a person or a group who has harmed me.

My thoughts were always that forgiveness is me giving up my right to extract revenge and not having people live rent free in my mind and heart.

Forgiveness is not always easy, but it is the best thing you can do for yourself.
I also say that when I forgive you, it does not mean you will continue to have access to me and anything that concerns me.
I can be nice to you but from a distance.

This is because some people will continue to use and abuse you if you continue giving them the access.

It does not mean I will continue to condone your behavior, nor will I forget it.

I remember it because it taught me a lesson. I forgive you and thank you.

God's word says that we should forgive, every time of everything that has caused us hurt.

If we have the fruits of the Spirit and walk in the Spirit, then forgiveness leads us to better understand people and things, it teaches us empathy and most of all we have compassion for the one who hurt us.

Those are words to live by.

Webster's dictionary defines Forgiveness – To stop feeling anger towards someone who has done you wrong, stop blaming someone. To give up resentment.

Allaboutgod.com put it so aptly:

Giving up my right to hurt you because you hurt me. It means to wipe the slate clean.

In areas where we must live with that person especially when it comes to family members or a spouse. For us to have that relationship restored, we must forgive each other. It is not always that forgiveness is deserved, but it must be treated as an act of love.

Forgiveness is a grace we have from God.

God gave so many instructions on forgiveness.

In **Matthew 6:14-15,** If we forgive others then God will forgive us. We forgive in obedience to God's word.

Sometimes depending on the hurt, it's hard to forgive. We need time to process.

The hurt runs deep, especially if that someone who has hurt us is someone close to us. Like a spouse, or family member. It takes some time but what is important that we should not let it fester.

Festering a hurt and not forgiving leads to bitterness.

Bitterness is a dangerous element to develop in our selves. There is a saying that bitterness is like drinking poison and expecting the other person to die.

Ephesians 4:31-32 says Let all bitterness, and wrath, and anger and evil speaking be put away from you. And be kind to one another.

By forgiving, it frees us emotionally and spiritually.

Forgiveness is a conscious effort, an act of obedience to God's will.

God will heal us emotionally from that hurt and pain.

As I said when it comes to a spouse and family members the relationship must be restored and for that to happen, forgiveness is necessary.

A lot of discussion should take place as to why it happened, and how the parties can make sure it does not happen again.

We are not perfect, and the act of forgiveness is always between us and God.

We are sinful, and we want God to forgive us, so in obedience to Him, we also must be like Him and forgive.

Remember His dying on the cross was not only for our salvation, but for the forgiveness of our sins.

Prayer for Forgiveness

Heavenly Father, I have wronged You in my words, in my thoughts and in my deeds.
Please forgive me. Teach me to be more like you.
Strengthen and sustain me.
Strengthen my walk with You.
Lord, help me always to be forgiving.
Teach me how to forgive and let go of all hurts so that I can be free from the weight of the pain.
Help me to throw the hurt and pain in the sea of forgetfulness just as You did for my sins.
Restore our relationship, bring healing to us both, and let us not hurt each other, but always treat each other with love, that same love that You have for us.
Lord, I release that person and thank You for removing the hurt and pain that I have.

In Jesus' mighty name, Amen

Notes

- All Scriptures came from the NKJ
- Webster's Dictionary was used for synonyms
- Impartation of the gifts of the Holy Spirit came from teachings that I learnt through various ministers of the gospel, through the bible, inspiration of the Holy Spirit.
- Bible Hub and the bible was used for research.

Much prayer and fasting went into the writing of this book.

It is my prayer that this book will bless you as much as it blessed me writing it.
That you learn from it, just as much as I learnt in writing it.
It was whilst writing this book, that I was going through many of the challenges.

Reading the bible daily will always be the source of help and inspiration.
It will always be the way God speaks to you.
It will either be in the still small voice, through the Holy Spirit and through His word.

He confirms His word with His servant. Isaiah 44:26

From my heart to yours,
Kathy

The Author

Kathy Lee lives in Florida. She is originally from Trinidad & Tobago, and her beautiful family – A son, his wife, and a Grandson; they live in Trinidad.

This is her first book, and, she has already completed a second book which will be published soon; and inspiration for her third is already being worked.

She hopes that the readers of her books are blessed and are ministered to through the scriptures, her experiences, as it was through her experiences that her books are being written.

Kathy developed a great love for God and her passion for ministering to others gives her great satisfaction.

As she says: "Being used by the Holy Spirit, is what gives me fulfillment".

04090052-00836298

Printed in the United States
by Baker & Taylor Publisher Services